Original title:
Winter's Slow Whisper

Copyright © 2024 Creative Arts Management OÜ
All rights reserved.

Author: Robert Ashford
ISBN HARDBACK: 978-9916-94-504-9
ISBN PAPERBACK: 978-9916-94-505-6

A Serenity of White

Snowflakes dance in the air,
They tickle my nose with flair.
As I trip on a hidden patch,
I land in a snowman match!

Sledding down a hill so steep,
I scream, oh dear! This is a leap!
With a crash into a snowdrift,
I become a frozen gift.

The Calm Before the Thaw

Beneath the pines, there's a hush,
Where squirrels dash with a rush.
Hot cocoa spills from little hands,
As snowmen plot their snowy plans.

In cozy homes, we brightly cheer,
While outside, the snowflakes leer.
They laugh at chilly winter's fate,
And plot for spring to take the bait.

Reflections on a Frozen Lake

On ice, the ducks play a game,
Skating 'round, oh what a shame!
One slips and takes a plummet,
Leaving all of us to plummet!

With penguin waddles all around,
My feet, they seem to leave the ground.
I twirl and spin with goofy grace,
Then lose my balance in this place.

The Yearning of Falling Flakes

Flakes fall down like popcorn light,
Making every rooftop bright.
A puppy leaps with pure delight,
Then rolls around, what a sight!

Children giggle with such flair,
As snowballs fly through the air.
Every throw met with a cheer,
As laughter rings through the cold air.

The Still Air's Reverie

The trees wear coats, oh so thick,
Squirrels ski on branches, what a trick!
Hot cocoa spills from the cheeky mug,
Chillin' out with a marshmallow bug.

Snowflakes dance like they're on parade,
I slip and slide, a toboggan's charade!
Chased by a snowman with a carrot nose,
I laugh so hard, my laughter just grows.

Dawn's First Chill

Morning creeps in, all frosty and bright,
Coffee's a friend, keeps my fingers tight.
My nose doesn't know whether to freeze or run,
I've got ice in my hair, oh isn't this fun?

The sun looks suspicious, peeking so low,
He's hiding behind clouds, putting on a show.
Pancakes stick like snow, while syrup's on strike,
I take a big bite, then slip on the pike.

Blossoms of Ice on Branches

The branches wear crystals like glitter so fine,
They sparkle and shimmer; oh, look at that line!
Birds in their jackets, looking quite bold,
Hitchhiking on hoodies, the new fashion sold.

Icicles drip-drop like a comical tune,
While snowmen gossip 'neath the light of the moon.
One tipped his hat; what a dapper old chap,
I laughed till I snorted, it felt like a nap.

Secrets Held in Snowdrifts

Behind every drift, there's a secret untold,
A squirrel's small fort with a stash of gold.
I try to approach with a careful peep,
And end up face-first in a pile so deep!

Snowballs are flying with giggles galore,
I duck just in time, but then hear a roar!
"Who threw that?" I cry with a grin on my face,
The answers come back like a playful race.

The Beauty of Hibernation

Bears snore loud, a symphony,
Blankets piled, a cozy spree.
Squirrels dream of acorn feasts,
Unaware of hungry beasts.

In the cave, a monster snoozes,
Out on ice, a penguin doozes.
Chubby cheeks and yawns galore,
Oh, the joys of an endless snore!

Veils of Ice Enchanting the Night

The moon peeks through frosty glass,
Snowflakes waltz as hours pass.
A raccoon dons a sparkly hat,
While critters join in a dance so fat.

Icicles are sparkling knives,
While penguins practice their high-fives.
Hare performs a limbo low,
In this chilly rave, they steal the show!

Soft Echoes Among the Snowdrifts

In snowdrifts soft, a rabbit bops,
Creating tracks like little hops.
A fox, confused, jumps every beat,
Then tumbles tail-first into a seat.

Snowmen stand with carrot noses,
Getting tired and striking poses.
With arms akimbo, they try to sway,
But melt a little more each day!

Frosty Reverberations

Icicles chime like festive bells,
Telling tales that no one tells.
Frosty gnomes with rosy cheeks,
Dance around in twinkling streaks.

Squirrels share their nutty jokes,
While snowflakes fall in silly cloaks.
It's a giggle, it's a cheer,
As winter plays its funny leer!

Veil of White over Gray

Snowflakes dance like tiny clowns,
Covering rooftops, schools, and towns.
Snowmen grin with carrot noses,
While kids hurl snowballs, oh how it doses!

Puddles freeze, the streets are slick,
A skating rink without a pick.
Laughter carries, echoes bright,
As sleds go tumbling with pure delight!

Serene Slumber Beneath the Stars

The moon peeks in, a silver tease,
While frost draws patterns on the trees.
Cups of cocoa fill our hands,
As we brave the cold, we take our stands.

Pajama parties round the fire,
With tales of snowmen that never tire.
Hot chocolate spills on fluffy socks,
As we ponder life and playful rocks!

The Soft Touch of Hibernation

Blankets piled like fluffy hills,
Even squirrels get their fill of chills.
Bears snooze deep with dreams so bright,
While we binge-watch shows through the night.

In the morning, it's bright and cold,
Fetching warm socks, oh the stories told!
Each cup of tea, a tiny cheer,
While icy drafts draw us all near.

Evergreen Memories in White

Pines adorned with snowy hats,
Squirrels in coats that look like spats.
Caroling voices sing from afar,
While we navigate drifts like a bizarre bazaar!

Each flake that falls tells a joke,
As frostbite gives way to the smoking cloak.
With cheeks aglow and laughter galore,
We'll stumble through snow, we'll laugh even more!

Stillness

The world has turned to pure white fluff,
As if the sky just gave up tough.
Trees wear coats of sparkling lace,
While squirrels race in a snowy chase.

Penguins in the park do play,
Chasing hats that flew away.
Snowmen laugh with carrot grins,
As they invite more snowball wins.

Wrapped in Cold

I bundled tight like a sausage roll,
Each step cracks ice as I stroll.
Frosty breath like dragon's puff,
Why's it so hard to look cool and tough?

Under layers I feel quite grand,
But can't find my mitten—darned if I can!
Running noses, what a sight,
In this chill, we find delight!

Silhouettes Beneath the Icy Moon

Shadows dance in the frosty light,
Jumping jacks in the snowy night.
Even the owls seem to laugh,
At penguins trying to take a path.

I spy foxes in their sleek coats,
Wobbling like they've got heavy boats.
Underneath the moon's bright smile,
Creatures frolic in cheeky style.

Dreams of a Snowy Landscape

I dreamt I built a castle tall,
But ended up with a snowball!
Each flake brings a fitting jest,
As snowmen sing, "We're the best!"

I asked a tree for some big advice,
It just chuckled, "Don't try to slice!"
The ground is soft like a marshmallow,
And I fell down—oh, what a fellow!

Together in the Frost-Bound Silence

We're twirling round like candy canes,
Slipping softly on the plains.
Friends might fall, but don't you pout,
"Did you freeze?" is what we shout!

We gather close with mugs of cheer,
Spilling cocoa, oh dear, oh dear!
As frosty tales fill the air,
Laughter echoes everywhere!

Whispers Between the Pines

In the quiet woods, trees wear white,
Squirrels skitter, what a sight!
Snowflakes dance like crazy bugs,
Pine trees chuckle, giving hugs.

The branches sway in silly glee,
As icicles play hide and seek, you see.
Beneath the blanket of powdery fluff,
Nature laughs, 'Isn't this enough?'

Cold noses peek from cozy coats,
Frosty breath in funny quotes.
Snowmen wobble, hats askew,
Each jolly giggle whispers, 'Boo!'

So join the fun, don't be shy,
Watch the world as frosty pies
Fall from rooftops, a snowy plot,
Even the robins laugh a lot!

Snowfall Serenade

With every flake that twirls and spins,
The rooftops wear their chilly skins.
Snowmen stand, proud and round,
Melting at jokes that are quite profound.

Penguins slide with goofy grace,
On frozen ponds, they find their place.
Chasing shadows, slipping by,
Each tumble met with a hearty sigh.

Hot cocoa spilled, marshmallows float,
In mugs that sing a funny note.
Frosty fingers try to knit,
But tangled yarn, oh what a fit!

As laughter echoes through the air,
Snowball fights bring shouts of care.
While fluffy friends all gather near,
The season's joy is loud and clear!

Midnight's Crystal Embrace

At midnight, snowflakes throw a ball,
With tiniest dancers having a ball.
The moon peeks in, a laughing guest,
Whispering secrets, quite unimpressed.

Outside, the world wears sparkly shoes,
Jingle bells hum winter's blues.
Footprints line up like a conga line,
Each clumsy step, a twist of vine.

Frosted windows, misty art,
Children giggle, all with heart.
A cat slips, then takes a leap,
In a snowdrift, falls in deep.

As glitter falls from skies so wide,
Underneath, all the snowflakes hide.
Each snowy night, a giggling chase,
In midnight's dance, there's endless grace!

Shivers of Delicate Silence

In brittle air, the silence cracks,
As little critters gather in packs.
Underneath the quilt, tales unfold,
With whispers shared, both brave and bold.

Icicles dangle, like tiny swords,
Ready for battles, waged with words.
Snowflakes crash like jokes so sly,
Each flurry giggles, 'Look, I fly!'

Puddles freeze, and laughter pools,
In whispered tales of winter's rules.
As snowmen scheme and bunnies hop,
Funny sounds won't ever stop.

So grab your hats, and join the show,
Where chilly winds blow laughter low.
In delicate silence, so much fun,
Under the snow, laughs weigh a ton!

The Quietude of Falling Feathers

In fluffy coats, the pigeons puff,
They strut about, acting quite tough.
Snowflakes dance, a clumsy waltz,
As kids slip down, their laughter exalts.

The ground is slick, a smiling foe,
Each step a gamble, a chance to show.
Snowballs fly with comedic aim,
Falling faces, yet all the same.

Sleds are racing, no time to wait,
Flying down hills, they tempt their fate.
Hot cocoa spills on mittens bright,
Every sip warms, just feels so right.

Yet here we are, in frosty cheer,
With frozen noses, we shed a tear.
For every slip and snowy fight,
Brings giggles under the pale moonlight.

Embrace of the Cold Moon

The moon hangs low, a big white pie,
We dig for warmth, a feeble try.
Chilblains are creeping up our toes,
In every laugh, a tickle grows.

Snowmen grin with coal-joke eyes,
Carrot noses, but they can't disguise.
As snowflakes land atop our hats,
We trade our stories and snowy spats.

Hot soup erupts with a steamy froth,
Feeding friends who've turned to sloth.
With hearty guffaws and chattering teeth,
We swaddle tight, no room for grief.

So let the chill play tricks and games,
In icy whispers, it calls our names.
With jolly hearts and cheeks aglow,
We frolic forth, despite the snow.

A Symphony of Soft Crystals

A sparkly coat on every tree,
The world's a stage for nature's spree.
Icicles drip in playful dribbles,
While critters play on frozen scribbles.

Snowball fights in the yard take flight,
Each furry toss feels just so right.
The wind's a jokester; watch your hat,
As snowflakes fall, we dance and spat.

Sleds zoom by with a whoosh and a cheer,
With laughter so loud, it's all we hear.
A snowflake lands right on my nose,
A giggling fit, nobody knows.

We bake warm cookies, fragrance divine,
While frosty noses wait in line.
The fire crackles as stories unfold,
In this chilly chaos, we're never cold.

Secrets Held in Frigid Air

The breath we breathe comes out like clouds,
A bumbled snowball hits the crowds.
When cheeks burn red from frosty play,
We laugh it off, come what may.

The trees wear shrouds of snowy lace,
Little ones wobble, some lose their face.
With sleds like rockets, they take to flight,
All our spirits are soaring bright.

Hot hands wrap 'round mugs, steaming high,
As we sip warmth while snowflakes fly.
Each giggle echoes through the glade,
In frozen antics, our memories made.

So here's to secrets that winter brings,
To silly antics and joyful flings.
With brightened hearts, we bravely dare,
To dance in the frosty, frigid air.

Chill of the Silent Night

The stars above are twinkling bright,
While squirrels wear hats, a silly sight.
Snowflakes dance upon my nose,
As penguins practice their waltz with toes.

The cold is nipping at my cheeks,
As I slip on ice, unplanned peak.
A snowman waves with a goofy grin,
I swear I heard him sing like a violin!

The moon is laughing, full of zest,
While old man winter takes a rest.
With every crunch beneath my feet,
I wonder who thought this was so sweet!

So let the flurries swirl around,
With playful tricks and laughter found.
In this frosty, jesting parade,
The chill of night, a stage well-played.

Frost-Kissed Secrets

I found a snowball, round and white,
I threw it first, what a delight!
But it hit a tree, and oh my gosh,
A raccoon peeked out, looking posh.

The ice on lakes is slick and mean,
But I skate for laughs, not for the scene.
I pirouette, and whoops, I fall,
That's one way to impress the snowball!

The whispers of frost, they giggle and tease,
Even the car tires slip with ease.
As I sip cocoa with marshmallows afloat,
A snowflake lands right on my coat.

The secrets of cold, they make me jest,
With every slip, I feel so blessed.
Embracing the frost, it warms my heart,
In this chilly play, I'm a goofy part!

Echoes of the Frostbound Forest

In a forest where owls hoot and freeze,
A rabbit wore boots, yes, if you please!
He hopped around with such a flair,
Making snow angels in his fluffy hair.

The branches creak, they sing and sway,
As snowflakes giggle, they dance and play.
An elk in a scarf, strutting by,
Looking like he's ready to fly!

A snowball fight with the trees and me,
They threw back leaves, as if to agree.
"Not fair!" I shout, as they shower snow,
In this frosty realm, laughter does glow.

With each crunch on this frozen ground,
The echoes of joy are all around.
In this chilly hideout, I find my cheer,
Amongst the frost, I shed no fear!

Quietude Beneath the Snow

Beneath a quilt of snowy fluff,
The world feels cozy, though it's tough.
A cat in a sweater, looking so grand,
Chasing a snowflake, oh, isn't it planned?

The air is still, yet there's a chuckle,
As a bird in boots gives a cheerful shuffle.
I sip hot tea, it's quite a toast,
To all the mischief, I love the most!

The snowman's hat flies off his head,
As the wind whispers dreams, silly instead.
Mittens on dogs, they frolic with glee,
In a world of wonder, come play with me!

So here's to the joys, both big and small,
In the space of snow, I'll have a ball.
With laughter and warmth, it's clear to see,
That beneath this frost, there's fun aplenty!

Gentle Touch of Frost on Earth

Chilly fingers dance on ground,
Tickling toes, I'm falling down.
Snowflakes giggle as they glide,
Sledding ducks go for a ride.

Icicle daggers hang above,
Melting hearts like frozen love.
Hot cocoa spills, a chocolate flood,
Face plants happen in the mud.

Scarves unwound in playful chase,
Slide on ice, oh, what a race!
Snowmen chuckle, hats askew,
Their carrot noses bid adieu.

Boots are soggy, socks are damp,
Freezing cheeks from frosty stamp.
Nature's jokes, a chilly tease,
Who knew cold could come with ease?

Frostbitten Lullabies

Pillow fights in puffy gear,
Hot tea spills, a little cheer.
Snowflakes fall like tiny toes,
Tickling noses, who knows?

Blankets wrapped, a cozy heap,
Squirrels dance, their nuts they keep.
Frosty breaths in sync we share,
Breath like smoke, we float in air.

Whispers soft, the wind reveals,
Laughter echoes, winter steals.
Snowmen frown, they melt away,
Just like me, I must obey.

Stuck indoors, with socks so bright,
Pretend the floor is ice tonight.
Giggles tumble in the cold,
Frostbitten stories, sweet and bold.

The Stillness Before Dawn's Embrace

Nighttime blankets all around,
Pin drop silence, what a sound.
Bunnies snooze in fluffy beds,
Dreaming dreams of carrot spreads.

Stars twinkle like frozen eyes,
Frosty plants in sleep disguise.
But I'm wide awake, oh dear,
Counting snowflakes, let's have beer!

Snowdrifts whisper, calling me,
A secret game, just wait and see.
Sneaking out to dance and play,
In the stillness, hip-hip-hooray!

Time for mischief, just a peek,
In the quiet, chaos peak.
Sleds and laughter take their flight,
As dawn stretches, what a sight!

Heartbeats in a Snow-Covered Landscape

Snowy hills, a wardrobe grand,
Woolly hats and scarves, oh, planned!
Slushy boots make splashes loud,
Charming snowballs, laugh out proud.

Penguins sliding down the hill,
Chasing joy, the air is still.
Frosty breath escapes our lips,
Time for fun and friendship trips.

Snow-covered trees wear costumes bright,
Sharing secrets in winter's light.
Icicles sparkle, stars on strings,
Jokes float around like snow in flings.

Gather 'round, the warmth we find,
In this frosty life, unwind.
Heartbeats echo, so alive,
In this chill, we truly thrive.

The Silence of Snowflakes

Snowflakes dance and twirl down,
Landing softly on the frown.
Mittens lost, oh what a chase,
Snowballs fly, now it's my face!

Sledding down a mountain steep,
Hitting bumps, the laughter's deep.
Hot cocoa spilled, what a sign,
Marshmallows float, looking divine!

Cold toes peek from underneath,
A snowman's hat, what a wreath!
Carrots for noses, oh so bright,
He's looking dapper, what a sight!

Chilly noses, cheeks so red,
Frosty hair, we call it "spread."
Let's catch snowflakes on our tongues,
And hum a tune that we all sung.

Breath of the Icy Night

A breath so cold, it makes you gasp,
Icicles hang like teeth from a clasp.
The stars above seem to snooze,
But wait, are those penguins in shoes?

Gloves are missing, hats askew,
Follow the footprints, they lead to stew!
My snowman's scarf is way too long,
But it looks stylish, like a song!

The moon's a giant, shining light,
Playing tricks with shadows tonight.
Snowball fights turn into mess,
Laughter hides from winter's press.

Sipping tea while toes are freeze,
Curl up tight, oh yes, please.
Hot water bottles, cozy dreams,
Who knew that frost came with such schemes?

Beneath the Frosted Veil

Trees like ghosts in the white sheet,
Footprints crunch beneath my feet.
Laughter echoes through the air,
Hot chocolate spills, but we don't care!

Slipping and sliding all around,
Trying to stand but hit the ground.
Snowflakes land on my dog's nose,
Chasing them is how this goes!

Frosted breath in a swirling game,
Every breath becomes a name.
Snow angels sprawled on frozen ground,
Only to find limbs lost, not found!

Snow forts built with artistic flair,
We throw a snowball, who's unaware?
Giggles burst like bubbles in cheer,
All's a snow-fun, bring on the year!

Hushed Hues of Dusk

The sky turns pink, a playful tease,
Frosty air nips at the knees.
Snowflakes glitter like treasure chests,
While we all wear our winter vests.

Pet squirrels dash, looking for snacks,
Beneath the trees, there's teddy's tracks.
Snow fights break out with not a care,
Heads buried deep in snowy hair!

Frosty windows tell tales untold,
Captured warmth beneath the cold.
What's that? A snowball, all for fun,
Who threw it first? Oh, it's begun!

Laughing loud as the sunset glows,
Chasing shadows, through dance we pose.
The dusk whispers secrets brisk and shy,
Closing the day with a snuggly sigh.

Treetops draped in Silent White

Treetops wear a frosty hat,
Squirrels slip and chat,
Birds in coats do shout,
"Where's the sun? We're out!"

Pinecones tumble with a clatter,
Snowflakes dance, what's the matter?
A snowman waves with a grin,
"Is that a carrot? Oh, chin!"

Icicles hang like sharp teeth,
"Time for hot cocoa, beneath!"
Yet the snowmen seem to sigh,
"Why can't we just fly high?"

Every branch in fluffy wear,
Bunnies hop, unaware,
In this frosty wonderland,
We laugh with snowballs in hand.

The Calm Beneath a Heavy Blanket

Underneath the layer thick,
Lies a world that plays a trick,
Animals snore in furry piles,
Dreaming of a sun's warm smiles.

Pillows made of snowflakes fall,
Quiet whispers, nature's call,
The ground is dressed, quite absurd,
"Who knew we'd nap with a bird?"

Shovels chase the children's feet,
Snowball fights become a feat,
Fingers numb, but hearts aglow,
"Bring on the cocoa, let's go!"

Shy are the steps on frosty trails,
As we slip with funny fails,
Warming up by fire's light,
Giggles echo through the night.

Shadows Under the Ice

Beneath the glaze, the shadows play,
Bright fish swim where skaters sway,
Twitchy toes on frozen lakes,
"Who knew ice could make such flakes?"

Laughter spills as friends glide past,
One trips, but who's got the last?
Snowmen chuckle with delight,
"Come join the dance in winter's sight!"

A dog dives in for a splash,
Watch him dash in a furious flash,
While ducks confuse the frosty grace,
With wobbly pirouettes, they race.

Underneath, the secrets sigh,
Nature's humor, oh my, oh my,
Laughter twirls through chilly air,
This time of year, we gladly share.

The Poetry of Frozen Streams

Streams like ribbons, now a dream,
Stillness wrapped in icy gleam,
As frogs sleep in a chilly hush,
"Will spring bring back the squishy mush?"

Froggies grin, while fish conspire,
"Let's write our book, let them admire,"
Words on ice, how funny that,
A fish with pen, just like a cat!

Every ripple frozen tight,
Makes us giggle with delight,
Tickled toes on frigid ground,
"Is there laughter all around?"

Nature's verses, crystal clear,
Woven tales we hold so dear,
In this hush, we find our song,
All together, we belong.

Murmurs of the Frigid Breeze

The breeze comes in with chilly glee,
Tickling noses, making us flee.
It laughs and giggles, spins around,
Chasing hats that tumble to the ground.

Hot cocoa's calling, sip it slow,
But look out now, here comes the snow!
It might be cold, but here's the catch,
Snowmen plotting their snowy batch.

With frosty fingers, snowflakes dive,
We build a fort, we're all alive!
Dodgeball with snowballs is the play,
Why stay inside on such a day?

Laughter echoes, we cheer and shout,
Life in frost is what it's about!
So wrap up tight, don't you feel that?
This chill's a prank—oh, look at that!

Crystals Dancing on the Air

Glittering gems from skies descend,
Little dancers that twist and bend.
They land on noses, socks, and hats,
As kids recall their playful spats.

Bundled folks with scarves so bright,
Run around with sheer delight.
The neighborhood echoes with squeals of joy,
As snowflakes fall on every girl and boy.

Snowballs fly like fuzzy missiles,
With laughter ringing through the whistles.
A crystal dance of pure chaos,
Who'll take a tumble? We just want to toss!

But wait a second, it's quite a sight,
The dog joins in, thinks it's a fight.
So let's all cheer, our spirits uplift,
These crystals twirling are nature's gift!

Midnight's Breath of Stillness

Under moonlight, shadows creep,
Where frosty secrets silently sleep.
The world's a canvas, pure and bright,
But squirrels plot mischief in the night.

The cold sings softly, hear it hum,
While playful flicks from branches come.
Snowflakes tumble without a care,
Like little shivers dancing in the air.

The stillness breaks with laughter clear,
As friends appear, we gather near.
Though breath is visible in the cold,
Our stories are the warmth untold.

So let's embrace this chilly fun,
With moonlit games we've just begun.
At midnight's hour, giggles arise,
In frozen tales beneath the skies!

Reflections in a Snowy Mirror

White blankets cover the world so wide,
Mirrors of snow, where giggles hide.
Each step we take leaves a mark,
As we stumble forth from dawn till dark.

Snowflakes crunching, quite the sound,
Echoes of laughter can be found.
With cheeks so rosy, faces aglow,
It's hard to keep from letting joy flow.

Belly flops into the drifting pile,
We roll and tumble with endless style.
"Let's make angels!" someone will say,
Watch us sparkle in our own way!

Reflecting fun in every flake,
An artful masterpiece we take.
Oh what joy, in a frozen dance,
In this mirror-land, we find our chance!

The Dance of Sleigh Bells in the Quiet

Sleigh bells jingle, tinkling fun,
While snowflakes join the silly run.
Mittens lost in a snowy race,
A frosty nose, a frozen face.

Hot cocoa spills as we take a sip,
Marshmallows float, a fluffy ship.
Laughter echoes, ice cubes fall,
We slip and slide, we trip, we sprawl.

The cold air bites, we frolic and cheer,
Snowman grins, he's had too much beer.
Carrot noses and scarves on tight,
Mischief making every cold night.

As the sun sets with a glowing hue,
We dance to the sounds of a frosty zoo.
Hot pies baking while outside we play,
Who knew the cold could bring such a fray!

Frosted Echoes

Snowmen wobble, they wear our hats,
While squirrels plot like sneaky rats.
Snowballs fly with laughter loud,
Who knew a chill could build a crowd?

Frosted windows, funny designs,
Faces peering through, lost in times.
Carrot sticks for little bites,
While sipping cocoa brings cozy nights.

Pants too snug from too many pies,
Every jolly jest, a surprise.
Slippers tossed in the snowy ground,
Who knew fun hid all around?

Giggles tumble as we play around,
Hop like penguins, fall on the ground.
In frosty whispers, joy ignites,
As we make magic of snowy nights!

Chilled Recollections

Hats that slide down to our chins,
Old stories shared of our winter sins.
Jackets zipped, the laughter flows,
Who knew cold could be such a show?

Icicles dangle, a dangerous foe,
But they glisten bright, putting on a glow.
A dog in snow, with leaps and bounds,
Chasing flakes that dance on the ground.

Stomping boots on frozen streets,
Frosty air, the heart skips beats.
Hot soup steams like a winter dream,
As we bowl snowballs, we're a team.

Fireplace crackles, tales grow grand,
Of icy mishaps, a jolly band.
With every frosty, cheerful twist,
Memories formed, we can't resist!

Surrender to Stillness

In blankets piled, we snuggle tight,
While snowflakes twirl in soft moonlight.
Hot hands warming, trying to fuss,
They're soft and toasty, without a rush.

The wind whispers softly, a cheeky tease,
Playful echoes bounce through the trees.
Snow chairs build where we sit and munch,
Muffins baked for a snowy brunch.

Furry hats and scarves galore,
Fall from heads as we head for the door.
Sliding down the slopes with glee,
Making moments, just you and me.

As laughter dances with the flakes above,
We find a rhythm, we find our love.
So here's to stillness, yet spinning fast,
In frosty fun, we'll make memories last!

Tranquil Moments Beneath the Storm

Snowflakes dance like silly sprites,
Tumbling down in fluffy tights.
Stick your tongue out, catch a few,
They taste of chilly, icy blue.

Puffs of powder all around,
Sledding down, I hit the ground!
Laughter echoes through the trees,
Avoiding bushes, dodging knees.

Furry friends in jackets stride,
Chasing tails with endless pride.
But when they roll, oh what a sight,
A snowball fight sparks pure delight!

So as the storms brew big and bold,
We find the joy from young to old.
A world of white, so vast, so bright,
Come join the fun, and hold on tight!

The Gentle Kiss of Cold

A nippy breeze with frosty breath,
Whispers of chill declare our death.
But we reply with warm hot cocoa,
Marshmallows dancing like a show, oh!

Scarves wrapped tight, but noses freeze,
Noses red like autumn leaves.
We giggle at the snot that drips,
A snowman formed from funny slips!

As snowflakes swirl in dizzy dance,
We slide around, a merry prance.
Each frosty bite ignites our glee,
Winter's quirks, oh, how we agree!

So sip that drink, don't be so bold,
This chilly spell can't break our hold.
We wrap in laughter, warm and tight,
Embracing joy in frosty light!

Numbed Hearts, Silent Thoughts

Frozen fingers, calloused toes,
Carrot noses on frosty foes.
In this chill, we find our fun,
Who knew cold could make us run?

Stumbling through a snowy maze,
We find our warmth in silly ways.
A snowball launch, a perfect shot,
And off we go, laughing a lot!

Gritty boots, a slippery slide,
We leak giggles, can't hide inside.
Even the icicles wear a grin,
A cold embrace, oh where have you been?

As nights grow long, and days are short,
Hearts remain warm in this chilly sport.
We may be numb, but spirits soar,
Laughing out loud, we all want more!

Ghostly Whispers of the Woods

Pine trees shiver, dressed in white,
Mumbling secrets through the night.
Owl hoots, a quirky tone,
Echoes back, though all alone.

Crimson berries peep from snow,
Tiny treats for a winter show.
The whoosh of wind, a playful tease,
What's hiding there among the trees?

Frosty fingers on my cheeks,
Nature's breath plays hide and seek.
The woods are alive, with chatter and cheer,
In every snowflake, winter's here!

So venture forth, let spirits gleam,
In the silence, find the dream.
With chilly whispers, laughter's found,
In this frosty playground, joy abounds!

Serenity in the Frosted Air

In a coat three sizes too wide,
The penguin parade takes a slide.
Snowflakes dance, a cheeky feat,
On fluffy clouds, they skip and beat.

Hot cocoa spilled on mittens bright,
Silly snowmen stand in delight.
With noses made of carrots found,
They wobble, giggle all around.

Chasing snowballs, laughter's ring,
Frosty breath like whispers sing.
A flurry of fun, frosty cheer,
Who knew snow could spread such beer?

So let us make snow-angel art,
While it's cold, let's warm the heart!
In frosted air, our joy's declared,
It's serious fun — so start prepared!

Softly Spoken Snow

A squirrel steals the last of bread,
While dressed in white, looks like a head!
Snowflakes whisper tales of cheer,
As hot tea steams in mugs held near.

The snowman with a crooked grin,
Waves hello with his twiggy chin.
Sledding down from hills so steep,
I tumble and go head over feet!

Icicles like teeth hang tall,
In icy jokes, they never fall.
The birds, they chirp with coats so bright,
Commenting on this chilly sight!

So wear your scarves and laugh out loud,
In this frosty, giggly crowd.
And when the snowflakes start to flow,
Let's leap and twirl in this soft glow!

The Quiet of Blizzards Past

Oh, the quiet when snow does play,
It tickles noses, runs away.
In the frosty hush, I sneeze,
Gathering snowflakes with much ease.

The dog leaps, not a care in sight,
Then rolls in snow, oh what a sight!
With every wag, a flurry stirs,
Making brief snowstorms, oh how it purrs!

Time stands still as the world turns white,
With laughter echoing, pure delight.
The little ones build forts so grand,
While parents chase them through crisp white land.

As the wind speaks softly, so light,
We giggle under blankets at night.
With hot fudge dribbled down my chin,
It's a comedy that will never thin!

Starlit Frost

Under starlit skies, a sight so cute,
A reindeer stuck in rubber boots!
He prances with a clumsy flair,
Dancing and slipping without a care.

Frosty whispers through the trees,
Tickle my nose like a playful breeze.
The moon sneaks peeks with laughter loud,
While capturing folly in a silver shroud.

Snowballs fly in a feathery drift,
Friends in giggles, it's the perfect gift.
As icicles jingle on homes nearby,
They harmonize with giggles that soar high!

So gather 'round the fire so bright,
With stories of snowball fights at night.
Under this canvas of chilly glee,
We chuckle and dance, forever carefree!

The Quieting of Earth

The snowflakes dance like little spies,
Flapping their wings in the chilly skies.
They sneak on rooftops, they giggle and glide,
While I sip cocoa, feeling quite spry.

The squirrels are wearing their snowflake hats,
Chasing each other like playful bats.
They slip and slide, oh what a sight,
As I chuckle softly at their acrobats.

The trees stand still, holding their breath,
Waiting for spring, but delaying their depth.
A snowman winks, with a carrot nose,
Dreaming of summer, how it loves to prep.

But as the chill wraps snugly around,
I find my laughter in the silence found.
For even in cold, a warm heart can glow,
As the world is muted, yet joy can abound.

Shadows on a Snow-Draped Path

Footprints in snow, a comical race,
With each little slip, I lose my grace.
The shadows stretch long, they prance and sway,
Like a dance of clowns at a winter's base.

A snow angel flops, looking quite absurd,
While my sleigh-ride skills are barely conferred.
With each hidden bump, I tumble and squeal,
Nature's slapstick, oh haven't you heard?

Laughter erupts as I shake off the cold,
In this frosty world, some stories are told.
Frosty the snowman just tripped on a rail,
Even the wind has now joined in the fold.

So here I tread on this path so bright,
In a mix of giggles and pure delight.
For when shadows play on this snow-draped route,
Every chilly chuckle feels perfectly right.

Lullabies of the Season

One night I heard a snowflake sing,
A melody wrapped in a sparkling ring.
It told tales of carrots and sledding fun,
Of rubber boots that squeeze like string.

Chubby cheeks and noses aglow,
The sound of laughter, a high-pitched flow.
The frozen puddles call out for skates,
Where giggles erupt in trials below.

A snowball war with fierce little foes,
Causing a blizzard of marshmallow glow.
But oops! A faceplant, what a grand sight,
Lullabies of chuckles, more laughs to bestow.

So when the chill wraps its arms round tight,
Let's gather the joy, don't hide it from sight.
For each frosty breath that we warm with a grin,
Is a melody sung in the hush of the night.

Ice-Kissed Reveries

Icicles drape like a comedy club,
With giggling droplets and frozen scrub.
I sip on my drink while the snowmen cheer,
And join in the fun as I rub the tub.

A skiff of frost on my sleeping cat,
He twitches in dreams of chasing a rat.
He's not a fan of this chilly surprise,
As I giggle at him in my cozy hat.

The carols are frosty, off-key, and sweet,
While penguins from movies dance on their feet.
I chirp like a bird at their silly calls,
As laughter cascades in the cold-ice repeat.

So let's savor the balm of this frosted night,
With jackets, hot drinks, and smiles so bright.
For even when ice tries to bite our toes,
We'll delight in the mirth of this chilly delight.

Soft Footfalls on Frozen Ground

Little snowflakes dance and twirl,
As I slide outside, a slip and swirl.
My dog in boots looks quite absurd,
He leaps like a gazelle, how bizarre this bird!

The path looks straight, but oh, so slick,
I take one step, and it's a quick flick.
The cold ground grins, it knows my fate,
As I wrestle with gravity, it's never too late!

Neighbors peek out, with mugs in hand,
They chuckle and point, it's quite unplanned.
Snowmen stand tall, with noses of carrots,
And I, the comedian, am quite the parrot!

So here's to the frosty, slippery fun,
When giggles and slips have just begun.
With snow on my face and laughter too,
Let's strut through the cold like it's nothing new!

The Secret Language of Cold

Chattering teeth, they speak in code,
Telling stories of the icy road.
My nose turns blue, a sight too sweet,
While bundled up, I shuffle my feet.

Squirrels wear jackets, it's quite the sight,
With winter gear, they're ready to fight.
Ice cream trucks sell hot cocoa now,
As penguins slide by, I take a bow!

Snowflakes giggle as they land on me,
I'm trying to dress, but it's no small fee.
Ear muffs and scarves, what a sight to behold,
Fashion statements made in the bitter cold!

So here in the frost, with whispers galore,
Every step taken on that crunchy floor.
I'll mimic the cold with a silly dance,
In this frozen world, let's take a chance!

Ghosts of the Glimmering Frost

Under the moon, the night is bright,
Ghosts of snowmen dance in the light.
With misplaced hats and scarves askew,
They wiggle and jiggle, just to amuse!

Footprints lead to nowhere, oh what a game,
As icy fingers play hide and seek, that's their aim.
The trees creak softly, they join in the fun,
Whispering tales of everyone!

A snowball fight with shadows in tow,
Laughter echoes where cold winds blow.
I throw a snowball, but it hits my pal,
Now that's how we start a snowman battle!

So let's toast to ghosts who glide with flair,
In this winter theatre, we're all on a dare.
With snowflakes and giggles, we play through the night,
In this frosty kingdom, we're all feeling bright!

Muffled Secrets in the Pines

Whispers of snowflakes fall from the trees,
As squirrels wiggle and dash in the breeze.
I tiptoe softly, but oh, that crunch!
The trees giggle back, it's quite the brunch!

Under a blanket of white so deep,
The world takes a nap, but not me, I leap.
Snowmen are watching, with sticks for arms,
They laugh as I stumble into their charms!

Pines wear coats of glistening white,
Their secrets held tightly, no need for fright.
As I make a snow angel in the cold,
I'm pretty sure I'm worth my weight in gold!

So let's sing to the snow, and dance with delight,
While the pines share stories all through the night.
With giggles and hugs wrapped in layers of fluff,
We're all winter warriors – isn't this stuff?

The Lullaby of Icebound Silence

In a world where snowflakes dance,
A squirrel slips, oh what a chance!
He tumbles down with fluffy cheer,
   Wishing cocoa would appear.

The rooftops wear a frosty hat,
While penguins waddle, oh so fat!
They slide and glide, with joyful glee,
As snowmen laugh, 'Come play with me!'

Icicles hang like a faux chandelier,
Dripping slowly, without any fear.
The garden gnomes are stuck in place,
They chattered loudly, 'What a race!'

In snowball fights, the giggles swell,
As the brave dogs bark, they ring the bell.
With chilly winds and playful shouts,
This frozen realm's where fun's no doubt.

Gentle Flurries of Time

A fluffy cat in a beanie hat,
Prowls through snow, oh fancy that!
Chasing flakes, with paws so light,
He dreams of fish in the frosty night.

Snow angels formed with clumsy flair,
Are sprinkled all through the frosty air.
While mothers sip their steamy brew,
Laughing at kids all turning blue!

Hot cocoa spills in giddy cheer,
As marshmallows float, they disappear!
The snowmen shrug, 'What do we care?'
It's just a game with ice to spare!

A sliding moose plays peek-a-boo,
Wobbling past with a clumsy crew.
But every slip and every fall,
Gives laughter that enchants us all.

Frosted Dreams in Twilight

In the twilight's snowy glow,
Bunnies dig in a dash and flow.
With tiny noses all aglow,
They hop and flop, putting on a show!

The stars above twinkle with glee,
As ice skaters spin, wild and free.
One takes a leap, lands in a heap,
Another giggles, 'Oh, count to three!'

A grumpy cat, adorned in frost,
Prowls around, feeling quite lost.
But then a snowshoe, a wild rhyme,
Makes him leap, oh precious time!

A chorus of critters, all in sync,
Flap their wings, give snow a wink.
With frosted laughs that drift and swirl,
This season spins a whimsical whirl.

Hushed Whispers of the Season

In the stillness, where silence reigns,
A penguin slips, oh such disdain!
A snowball whizzes, oh what a throw,
While wise owls giggle, stealing the show.

With cheeks aglow, kids rush outside,
Building igloos with a snowball slide.
While dogs run wild in a snowy chase,
Each leap a dance, a snowy embrace!

Snowflakes twirl like a feathered song,
As frosty fingers dance along.
A teddy bear hides, just peeking out,
Wishing for hugs, not a winter drought!

So let's toast to frosty frolics bright,
And cuddle close in the soft twilight.
For each giggle and cheerful cheer,
Brings warmth and joy, the season's steer.

A Caress of Crystal Dreams

Frosty flakes dance on my nose,
Sneezy chimneys, where laughter grows.
Snowmen wobble, hats askew,
They're plotting mischief, just like you!

Icicles hang like pranks on hold,
With each drip, there's a story told.
I slip and slide, oh what a sight,
Adventures chase me, day turns to night!

Cocoa spills, a chocolate fight,
Mittens tangled in sheer delight.
Chilly giggles erupt like cheer,
As snowflakes whisper, "Joy's right here!"

The world transformed, a comic scene,
Snowy shenanigans, a frosty dream.
So here's to laughing, come join the spree,
In this frozen realm, wild and free!

Whispers of the Glacial Wind

The frosty breeze plays hide and seek,
With bobbing scarves, it feels quite cheek!
Snowball fights break the chilly charm,
Dodging snowflakes, we're safe from harm!

Wobbly kids on sleds descend,
Behind them, snowmen stand and defend.
Giggles and tumbles fill the air,
As warmth from laughter replaces care!

Hot pies cooling near icy doors,
Grandma's secret recipe that soars.
Stealing bites, with crumbs in hand,
Who needs the sun? We're a lively band!

Glacial whispers, teasing the night,
With every flake, a chuckle in sight.
So grab a mug, let the fun begin,
In this dance of frost, we'll laugh and grin!

Twilight's Embrace

As daylight fades with a timid blush,
Furry creatures in a snowy hush.
Chase the shadows, tickle the dusk,
In the crisp air, there's a joyful musk!

Snowflakes twirl like little clowns,
Poking fun on fluffy gowns.
A snow angel lands with a flump,
In a dramatic frosty thump!

Pine trees don their crystal coats,
While birds share jokes with little notes.
Under twinkling stars, we dance and sing,
Winter's stage, the merriest fling!

So gather round, let stories flow,
Of fanciful nights in the soft moon's glow.
For even in the icy embrace,
Laughter finds its rightful place!

Glints of Silver in Dim Light

The pale light glimmers on a frozen lake,
Where skaters glide, making no mistake.
They wobble and twirl with flair and grace,
With giggles echoing in the chilly space!

Frosty toes tucked in furry socks,
Tales of snowmen with funny clocks.
They laugh at the sun, while sipping tea,
In a world where funny is the key!

Hats and scarves come to life in glee,
While giggling snowflakes flicker and flee.
Every step crunches beneath our feet,
In this land of chilly, playful beat!

So let the silver sparkle and gleam,
With laughter that flows like a twinkling stream.
For in this realm, joy takes flight,
In the beautiful colors of the frosty night!

The Time of Cuddled Dreams

Under blankets piled so high,
I fear I might take off to fly.
Socks are missing, how bizarre,
Did they escape to distant stars?

The cat's got claims on half my bed,
While I'm stuck, a pillowhead.
The dog just snorts and takes a nap,
I'm left to fend beneath this flap.

Tea and cookies, my best friend,
Until crumbs invade my cozy end.
A blanket fortress, I declare,
Turns out I've knitted quite a lair!

So let the cold outside conspire,
Inside, we'll be warm, never tired.
Each cuddle's a laughter, pure delight,
Let's giggle through this frosty night!

Echoing Through the Frozen Stillness

Snowflakes dance like little girls,
Twisting, twirling, with snowy twirls.
Yet my car's stuck, oh what a sight,
Wipers frozen, took off in flight.

The neighbors build their icy king,
While I just grumble, it's a bad fling.
My snowman's missing a carrot nose,
Rumor has it, he ate it, who knows?

Sledding's fun until I crash,
Landed hard, oh what a splash!
If you hear a thump or shout,
Just know I'm fine—maybe out and about.

So raise a cup to frozen days,
Let's laugh at winter's silly ways.
In the stillness, we'll find our cheer,
With ice jokes ringing loud and clear!

Sentiments Encased in Ice

Icicles hang like little spears,
As I sip cocoa between my ears.
Outside, the world has turned to frost,
But hot chocolate makes it worth the cost.

When snow shoveling turns to play,
I toss a snowball, my aim's okay!
Laughter echoes as I take my stance,
Ready for this frosty dance.

Oh, dear mittens, where have you gone?
One's on my right, the other's drawn.
It's a mystery wrapped in warm knit,
Perhaps that's where your partner will sit.

So let's embrace this chilly spell,
With quirky tales we'll tell so well.
For in this icy land of fun,
The laughter's melting—one by one!

Frosted Sonnet of the Night

With each crunch of shoes on the ground,
We're masters of snow, let's jump around!
The moonlight sparkles, a sparkly show,
   Turns my backyard to a frosty glow.

Yet here I stand, a frosty mess,
My scarf's tied wrong, I must confess.
I roll a snowball and toss it high,
–Oops! There goes the laundry—oh my!

   Under the stars, I trip and slide,
   With each tumble, I chuckle wide.
   Snowy faces, joyful cries,
   As winter's antics fill the skies.

So gather 'round for this silly rite,
In frozen streets, we dance tonight.
Let tickles and giggles take their flight,
   Embracing joy in chilly delight!

The Solitude of the Snow-Covered Hearth

The fire crackles without a care,
A marshmallow's dance in the frosty air.
The chair's too soft, it swallows me whole,
I'll need backup to save my soul!

The cat's plotting a warm take-over,
As I dodge snowballs thrown by my brother.
With hot cocoa in hand, I raise a toast,
To the fluffiest blankets, I love the most!

Outside, the snowflakes put on a show,
But inside, I'm stuck with this silly glow.
My socks are mismatched, but who cares a bit?
In this cozy chaos, I choose to sit!

So here's to the quilt of white outside,
To hot cider, sledding, and laughter wide.
In this frosted world, we dance and twirl,
Finding joy in the chill, isn't life a whirl?

Inscription on the Ice

Ice skates thrumming like a chiming bell,
I zig, I zag, but I cannot quell.
A graceful glide turns into a spin,
Flat on the ice, oh where do I begin?

The sign tells me, "Just stay on your feet!"
But here I am, stranded, a chilly treat.
A penguin parade if you squint just right,
With giggles exploding in frosty delight.

Snowmen plotting as we crash their party,
With carrot noses, they look so hearty.
But little do they know, I've packed some snow,
For a snowball battle, let's see how they go!

So if you see my wild, flailing arms,
Just know I'm dancing, avoiding the harms.
Life's icy adventure, all is not lost,
In each silly slip, we find joy at the cost!

A Palette of Winter Solace

Crimson berries hang on the frosted vine,
With each step crunching, a sound so divine.
I tripped on a mound in this snowy spree,
Now my face is a canvas, oh woe is me!

Pine trees adorned like holiday cheer,
Whispering secrets, can you hear?
We throw snowballs, but ducks take flight,
As we laugh at the frostbitten birds in their plight.

The scarf's wrapped tight, but my nose peeks through,
With cheeks like cherries, oh what can I do?
We sip on hot chocolate, marshmallows afloat,
While laughter and giggles dance in the coat.

So let's celebrate this brisk, funny spree,
With snowmen and swirls, and laughter in glee.
A palette of winter, bright and absurd,
In this wintry tableau, joy is assured!

Frosty Musings

The world outside is a frozen dream,
And I'm huddled close, just me and my cream.
The pancakes are flipping, oh what a sight,
I think I've cooked them until they took flight!

The ice on the window's a mystical art,
Jack Frost's doodles, oh he's quite the heart.
But I'm stuck inside, wearing socks with flair,
While snowmen giggle at my fuzzy hair.

A snowstorm's brewing, we're ready for fun,
With games and hot cider, let's get this done!
I step from the door, toes diving in snow,
But I slip and slide, just like a pro!

So here's to the chill, the laughter, the cheer,
With friends by the fire, the season is dear.
In frosty musings, let joy be our guide,
In the quilt of the cold, let's dance and abide!

Threads of White Beneath the Stars

A frosty hat on a snowman's head,
He looks like he's had too much bread.
Penguins in coats made of fluff and cheer,
Slipping and sliding, oh dear, oh dear!

The trees wear blankets, all snowy and bright,
Yet squirrels throw parties, what a silly sight!
They dance with acorns, stash them with glee,
While snowflakes giggle, oh won't you see?

Bright stars above with a twinkle, a wink,
Joking with snowflakes that fluff up the pink.
They swirl around, it's a cosmic parade,
Every twirl sends a chill, yet we're still not dismayed!

So let's raise a mug, filled with cocoa delight,
And dream of snowmen who dance through the night.
In this chilly sphere, laughter we'll find,
As we tiptoe through snow, oh so lightly aligned!

The Subtle Dance of Chill

A dance-off with frost, come take a chance,
While icicles wiggle, they join in the dance.
Giggling snowflakes whirl around in delight,
As snowmen compete, their noses in sight.

The pets in their jackets prance 'round the yard,
Chasing their tails, it's surprisingly hard.
Canines in scarves, looking dapper and neat,
Slip on the ice, oh, what a funny feat!

The wind plays a tune, a whimsical sound,
It tickles the trees, making branches bow down.
The chill whispers secrets, though none can be told,
Except for the laughter that makes us feel bold!

So gather your friends and wear your best hat,
Let's build some grand forts and have a good spat.
With snowball surprises and jokes on the side,
We'll celebrate chill with our hearts open wide!

Shadows Under the Winter Sky

In the pale moonlight, shadows start to creep,
Sledding raccoons, sneaking off to sleep.
With twinkling eyes, they peek from the trees,
Riding through snow with an effortless ease.

A polar bear wearing a fuzzy blue coat,
Winks at a rabbit who's learning to float.
They giggle together, as they slide and glide,
Dodging snowflakes that dance, they can't seem to hide.

Yet here comes a penguin, or so it appears,
With a wiggle and slide, he brings forth the cheers.
He slopes down the hill on a tuna-shaped sled,
Shouting, "This winter, I won't go to bed!"

In shadows of fun, where the laughter roams free,
We chase after tales, as wild as can be.
So let's share our giggles 'neath this frosty bright sky,
For joyful are moments when silly birds fly!

A Tale of Ice and Solitude

An ice cube sat, feeling lonely and blue,
Wishing for friends, a quart or a crew.
He slipped and he slid on the counter so grand,
With no one to dance with, he hatched a bold plan.

He called for a kettle, "Come join in the fun!
Let's brew up some laughter before I am done!"
The kettle replied with a whistle, a gleam,
"I'd love to join, let's stir up a dream!"

They twirled on the counter, a frothy ballet,
Spilling some sugar along the grand way.
With a sprinkle of cinnamon, oh what a sight,
Ice cubes and kettles, dancing with delight!

So here's to the friendships that blossom anew,
In the cold winter air, where warmth comes in view.
May we find joy in the quirkiest friends,
And laugh through the cold, as the silly never ends!